W9-ATZ-258

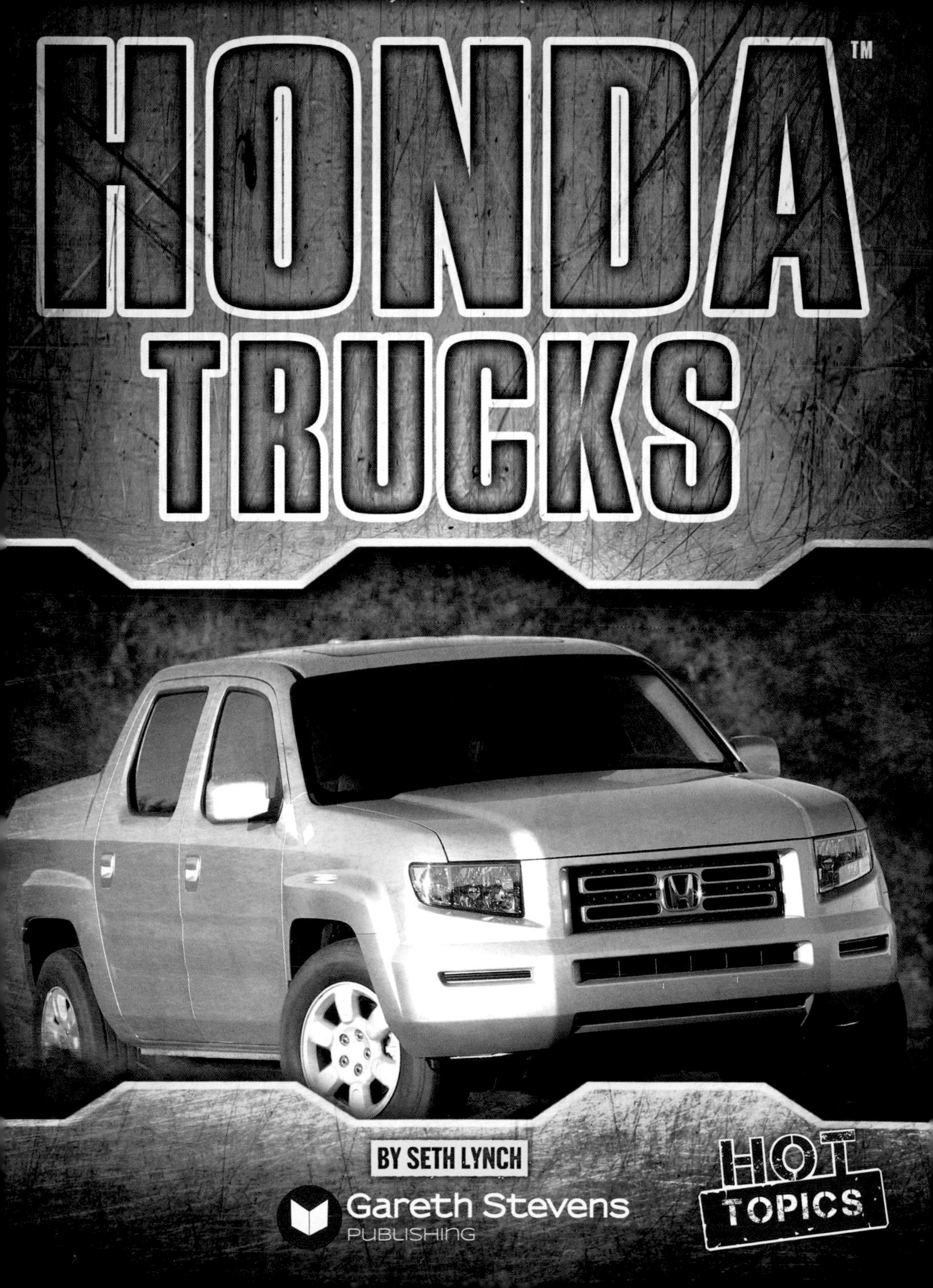

TOUGH TRUCKS
HONDA™
TRUCKS
BY SETH LYNCH
Gareth Stevens
PUBLISHING
HOT
TOPICS

**Please visit our website, www.garethstevens.com. For a free color catalog of all our high-quality books, call toll free 1-800-542-2595 or fax 1-877-542-2596.**

**Library of Congress Cataloging-in-Publication Data**

Names: Lynch, Seth, author.
Title: Honda trucks / Seth Lynch.
Description: New York : Gareth Stevens Publishing, [2019] | Series: Tough trucks | Includes index.
Identifiers: LCCN 2018023554| ISBN 9781538230374 (library bound) | ISBN 9781538231524 (pbk.) | ISBN 9781538231531 (6 pack)
Subjects: LCSH: Honda trucks--History.
Classification: LCC TL230.5.H65 L96 2019 | DDC 629.223/2--dc23
LC record available at https://lccn.loc.gov/2018023554

First Edition

Published in 2019 by
**Gareth Stevens Publishing**
111 East 14th Street, Suite 349
New York, NY 10003



Designer: Katelyn E. Reynolds
Editor: Kristen Nelson

Photo credits: Cover, p. 1 Business Wire via Getty Images; cover, pp. 1–32 (background) phiseksit/Shutterstock.com; pp. 5, 30 (2017) Steve Lagreca/Shutterstock.com; p. 7 Takeyoshi Tanuma/The LIFE Picture Collection/Getty Images; pp. 9, 30 (1963) 韋駄天狗/Wikipedia.org; p. 11 Mytho88/Wikipedia.org; pp. 13, 30 (1964) Kzaral (https://www.flickr.com/photos/32811347@N08) Cropped by uploader Mr.choppers/Wikipedia.org; p. 15 © iStockphoto.com/Tramino; p. 17 pim pic/Shutterstock.com; pp. 19, 30 (2006) Bryan Mitchell/Getty Images; pp. 21, 30 (2014) Seyit Aydogan/Anadolu Agency/Getty Images; p. 23 Daniel Acker/Bloomberg via Getty Images; pp. 25, 30 (2018) Paul Albrecht/Wikipedia.org; p. 27 Jim Denkert/Wikipedia.org; p. 29 Darren Brode/Shutterstock.com



Printed in the United States of America

CPSIA compliance information: Batch #CW19GS: For further information contact Gareth Stevens, New York, New York at 1-800-542-2595.

# CONTENTS


Today's Truck 4

Honda History 6

Mini Trucks 10

Time of Growth 14

Introducing... 18

New Ridgeline 22

Trims 26

Racer! 28

Honda Trucks Through History 30

For More Information 31

Glossary 32

Index 32

# TODAY'S TRUCK

Honda hasn't been making modern pickup trucks for very long. But since the Ridgeline was introduced, the company has worked hard to make each year's truck better than the last. Today, Ridgelines are known for driver comfort and a great look!

RIDGELINE

2017 Ridgeline

## FULL THROTTLE!

A pickup is a truck that has a cab, or driver's area, and a bed on the back that has low sides.

# HONDA HISTORY

Honda was founded in Japan in the 1940s. The first **vehicle** it produced was a motorized bicycle. Soon, Honda became well known for making motorcycles. By the 1960s, it was one of the biggest motorcycle makers in the world!

## FULL THROTTLE!

In 1949, Honda's cofounders Soichiro Honda (pictured above) and Takeo Fujisawa introduced the company's first motorcycle, which they had named the "Dream."

During the late 1950s, Honda started working on **designs** for other automobiles, or vehicles. One of these was a mini truck. It had a cab and bed like a pickup truck. The prototype, or first model, for the mini truck was finished during the summer of 1960.

T360

## FULL THROTTLE!

Fujisawa wanted to make a mini truck because he thought people mostly wanted to buy **commercial** automobiles.

# MINI TRUCKS

Honda continued to make the mini truck better until 1962. That year, the T360 mini truck was first seen at the Japan National Auto Show. The first T360s were sold in August 1963.

S500

## FULL THROTTLE!

Honda **developed** two sports cars at the same time they were working on the T360. One of them, the S500, came out a few months after the T360.

In 1964, Honda introduced a slightly bigger—but still mini—truck called the T500. It could hit speeds up to 65 miles (105 km) per hour. Neither the T500 nor the T360 were sold in the United States.

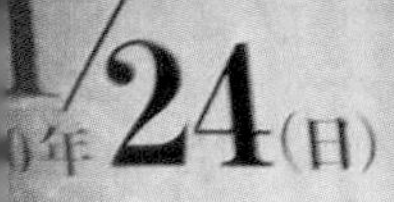

T500

## FULL THROTTLE!

Very few T500s have ever made it to North America. Collectors say there are only around three in the United States!

# TIME OF GROWTH

Honda didn't put out a new truck for many years. However, the company was growing during this time. Honda began selling its automobiles in the United States, where its motorcycles had been selling since the 1950s.

1970s Civic

## FULL THROTTLE!

Honda opened an automobile factory in the United States in 1979, making it the first Japanese car company to do so.

Honda became known for well-made, **efficient** cars. They put out the first **hybrid** electric car to be sold in the United States in 1999. By the late 1990s, Honda began making crossover vehicles like the CR-V, too.

1990s CR-V

## FULL THROTTLE!

A crossover is a vehicle built on a **platform** of a car but meant to carry more than a standard car. It's a word sometimes used in place of "sport utility vehicle," or "SUV."

# INTRODUCING...

In 2005, Honda introduced its first truck available in North America: the Ridgeline. The 2006 Ridgeline was built on the platform of the Honda Odyssey, a minivan. This gave it a comfortable ride many drivers liked.

2006 Ridgeline

## FULL THROTTLE!

In 2006, the Ridgeline won *Motor Trend* magazine's Truck of the Year award.

The 2006 Ridgeline had a **V6 engine** and could reach 60 miles (96.6 km) per hour in just 8.5 seconds. The bed had lots of space for camping or fishing gear, or for any load up to about 1,500 pounds (680 kg).

2014 Ridgeline

## FULL THROTTLE!

Honda stopped making the Ridgeline in 2014. Its sales were down and it needed a new look.

# NEW RIDGELINE

In 2017, Honda reintroduced the Ridgeline. The truck was slightly wider and longer but weighed less. Its V6 engine could now reach 60 miles (96.6 km) per hour in 7.3 seconds.

2017 Ridgeline

## FULL THROTTLE!

The redesigned Ridgeline had some cool features, including speakers in the truck bed and a big trunk hidden in the bed.

The 2019 Ridgeline can come with two-wheel drive or all-wheel drive. Ridgelines with two-wheel drive can pull up to 3,500 pounds (1,588 kg). Those with all-wheel drive can pull up to 5,000 pounds (2,268 kg)! All Ridgelines come with a V6, 280-**horsepower** engine.

2018 Ridgeline

## FULL THROTTLE!

All-wheel drive means the engine sends power to all four wheels. Two-wheel drive means the engine sends power to only the front wheels or the back wheels.

# TRIMS

Ridgeline trim levels build on one another. The higher level a driver buys, the more features they will have. The Ridgeline Black Edition has all the cool features of other trim levels as well as a special black design inside and out.

2017 Ridgeline Black Edition

## FULL THROTTLE!

A trim level is all the different features, parts, or abilities available for a type of vehicle.

Honda makes a Ridgeline for racing, too! This truck looks a lot like the Ridgeline and has a similar V6 engine. However, the racing engine puts out 550 horsepower! The Ridgeline Baja Race Truck takes part in off-road and desert races.

Ridgeline Baja Race Truck

## FULL THROTTLE!

In 2015, the Ridgeline Baja Race Truck took part in its first Baja 1000 race. It completed all 821 miles (1,321 km) of the race. Not every truck can!

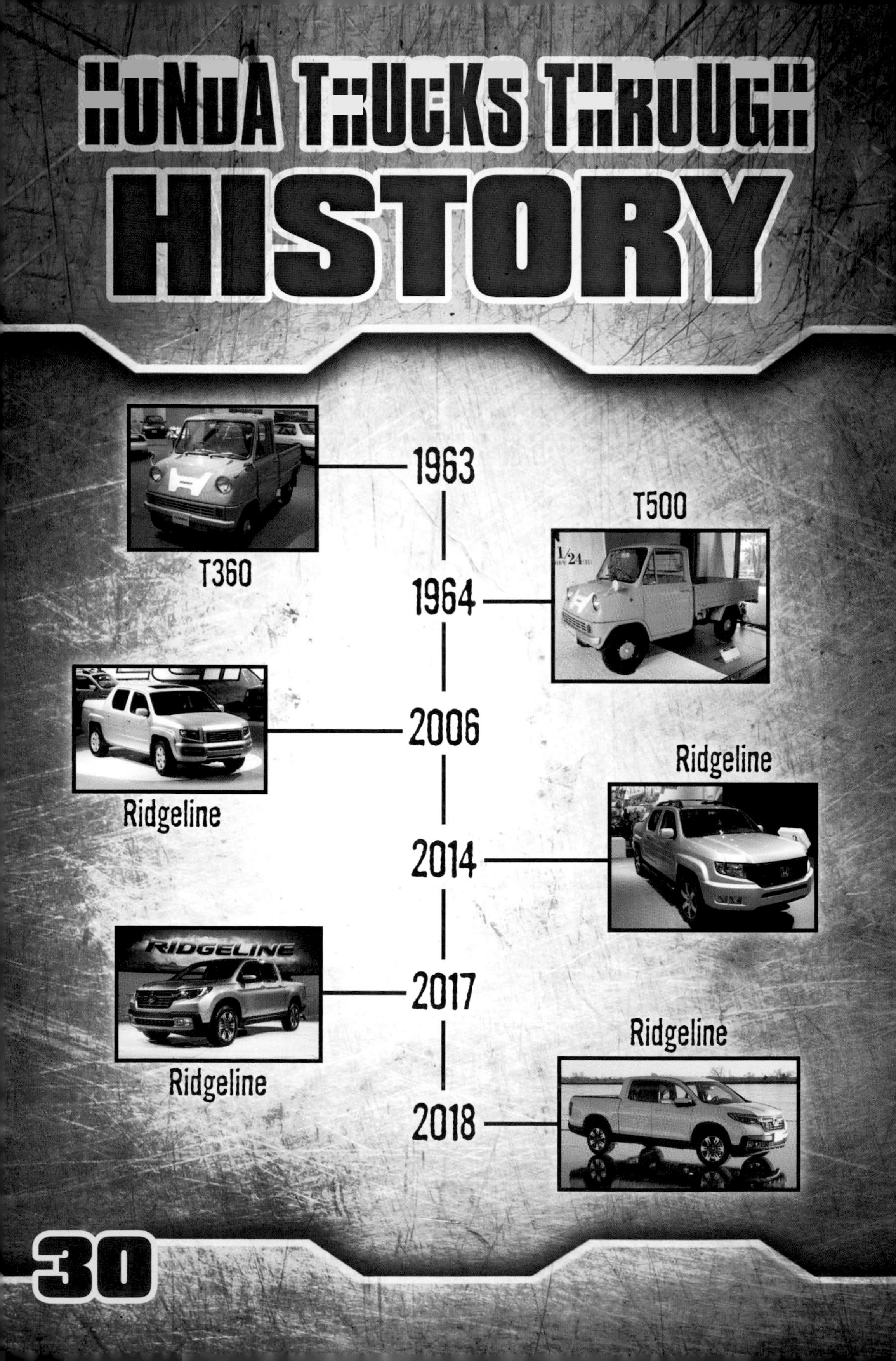
HONDA TRUCKS THROUGH
HISTORY
1963
T360
T500
1964
2006
Ridgeline
Ridgeline
2014
RIDGELINE
2017
Ridgeline
Ridgeline
2018

# FOR MORE INFORMATION

## BOOKS

Fishman, Jon M. *Cool Pickup Trucks*. Minneapolis, MN: Lerner Publications, 2019.

Mack, Larry. *Honda Ridgeline*. Minneapolis, MN: Bellwether Media, Inc., 2019.

Weston, Mark. *The Story of Car Engineer Soichiro Honda*. New York, NY: Lee & Low Books, Inc., 2017.

## WEBSITES

**The Best Reasons to Choose the Ridgeline**
*automobiles.honda.com/ridgeline*
Explore even more features of the Honda Ridgeline.

**Pickup Trucks 2018–2019: The Best and the Rest**
*www.caranddriver.com/best-pickup-trucks*
Read about other popular pickup trucks on the road today.

# GLOSSARY

**commercial:** having to do with the buying and selling of goods and services

**design:** the pattern or shape of something. Also, to create the pattern or shape of something.

**develop:** to create over time

**efficient:** having to do with the most effective or purposeful way of doing something

**horsepower:** a unit used to measure the power of an engine

**hybrid:** able to run on electricity and gasoline but using one or the other at a time

**platform:** the basic frame of a vehicle

**V6 engine:** an engine, or a machine that makes power, with two banks of three cylinders arranged in a V shape

**vehicle:** an object used for carrying or transporting people or goods, such as a car, truck, or airplane

bed 5, 8, 20, 23

engines 20, 22, 24, 25, 28

horsepower 24, 28

hybrid cars 16

Japan 6, 10

mini trucks 8, 9, 10, 12, 13, 30

motorcycles 6, 7, 14

Ridgeline 4, 5, 18, 19, 20, 21, 22, 23, 24, 25, 26, 27, 28, 29, 30

Ridgeline Baja Race Truck 28, 29

trim levels 26, 27

United States 12, 13, 14, 15, 16